POETIC

MEMOIRS

S. S. MILLER

BK Royston Publishing
Jeffersonville, IN 47131
http://www.bkroystonpublishing.com
bkroystonpublishing@gmail.com

© Copyright – 2025

All Rights Reserved. No part of this book may be reproduced, stored in a retrieval system, or transmitted by any means without the written permission of the author.

Cover by: Elite Covers

ISBN-13: 978-1-967282-70-8

Printed in the United States of America

Dedication

I dedicate Poetic Memoirs to you (the reader). I was called to deliver my thoughts, life encounters, and different concepts. I was given a gift to give away. I was told by sharing my experience. It would empower others. To be their true authentic selves. You are not alone. You have finally found your tribe. And through these words we are forever bonded.

Acknowledgements

I would like to think any and everyone who helped me along this journey. Thank you to all my family, friends, and publisher. You are appreciated.

Table of Contents

Dedication	iii
Acknowledgements	iv
Introduction	vii
Poems	1
Let Me	2
Confidence	3
Stand By Me	5
Pinocchio's Sarcasm	7
Dreams	9
What Is	11
Life	12
Soul	13
True Colors	15
Withdrawals	17
Secret Feelings	19
Personal Problems	21
Nothing But the Best	24
Keep Away	26
Clownz	28
Reruns	30
A Man's Mental Health	32
I'm Okay	33
Emotional Silence	35
Depression	37

Self-Destruct	39
Self-Betrayal	41
Accountability 2	42
L'S	44
Waiting on God	46
I Am Capable	48
Her Love Story	51
Lady in Disguise	53
Connection	55
Animated	56
Communicate Don't Conversate	59
A Creative Farmer	61
Giving Thanks	63
What Would You Do	65
Amerikkka	67
Injustice	69
Memorial Day	71
Labor Day	74
Black History	76

INTRODUCTION

POETIC MEMOIRS is a series of poems based on life experience and my perspective. Some could even be considered a collection of journal entries. Each one is unique and different from the others. Most have the date and time to put you in that moment with me, and takes you through a unique journey of this poet's trials and tribulations. These poems speak on everything, from personal issues to world views, and relationships included.

I hope that by sharing my views and opinions, someone is helped through a difficult situation. For me, poetry is my therapy, and it brings me clarity. It is also a gift from the source energy. It was given to me to give to you. The goal is for you to take away something meaningful from this book that will stick with you. If you enjoy reading for fun, that's ok too. If you're just a fan of poetry, then you'll love this book.

"POEMS"

JANUARY 30, 2023

10:37 P.M.

Poems are beautiful expressions of our DNA

Soundtracks narrating our story

Verbal scabs I pick

Revisiting heartache and suffering

My pen bleeds

Sharing with you pieces of me

Like the Lord's supper

LET ME...
FEBURARY 4, 2024
11:05 A.M.

Let me mend your heart

Let me water your soul

Let me be the one

To help you grow

CONFIDENCE

AUGUST 13, 2022

9:50 A.M.

To feel, believe, and have a firm trust

Keep going

You must

Even if it's not

Making no dust

Opinions are blocked

By a divine force field

I'm smiling on a mission

There is nothing to discuss

I see it clear

Whether they do or not

I prepare, strategize

Plan and plot

Equipped and organized

You can feel it in my vibe

See it in my eyes

Self-assured confidence

On the surface

Infatuated love

A weird type of lust

Fueled by purpose

The outcome is colossal

So, yes, sometimes

I do get nervous

Not only am I manifesting my dreams

I am doing and providing a service

"STAND BY ME"

FEBRUARY 17, 2020

12:03 a.m.

Would you stand by me

If I were surrounded by devils?

Would you stand by me

If there was no way out?

And we had to jump

From the top level

If I were on the run

From the government and

Had one bullet left in my gun

If they wanted to assassinate

And crucify me

Would you stand by me?

If it were me against the world

Could I depend on you

All the way to the end?

Will you remain true

If it's a hundred guns aimed at us?

Could you stand by me

In complete trust

If you overheard people

Saying I was crazy?

Would you have my back

Stand up for me or be shady?

Would you go to hell and back

If I promised Heaven

Was at the end of that

For worse or for better?

Will you stand by me

Through whatever?

PINOCCHIO'S SARCASM

FEBRUARY 2, 2022

10:50 P.M.

The world has always been

A wonderful place

All love and no hate

No racism

We are all one race

Everyone is honest and real

No one at all is fake

No one kills, lies, or steals

Not even set traps with bait

Everyone hugs and gives

No one is greedy or just takes

The world is full of Care Bears

You are never

Surrounded by sneaky snakes

Everyone speaks truth

Has warmth for humanity

Times two

The powers that be

Are here for one reason

To take care of you

Feed you the best

Most importantly, get that

Stress off your chest

The population has never

Been used as pawns

In a sick game of chess

Not once has it been a tragedy

And cops, on no occasion,

Murder people who

Look like me

As far as I can see

DREAMS

JULY 6, 2022

10:17 P.M.

When I dream

I relax

And I drift off into the abyss

Of infinite multiple realities

I leave my fingerprint

Most nights my dreams are unalike

Some were reoccurring

Every detail is a memory

Staying with me

Some people and places

Have that effect where you hate to leave

Or don't want to go back

I lost count

Of how many sunrises I woke up wet

from a bucket of cold sweats

PTSD is known for that

Some realms I visit I can't get back

And I miss it

Many moons I spend searching

Lucid dreaming in a hypnotic state

I am a god

I grand rise

I do not awake

There's nothing good about mourning

I hate to see my people's soul shake

WHAT IS

JULY 23, 2022

12:15 A.M.

"What's the meaning of life?" A voice says

I stand on the porch

Gazing into the sky at night

Mind blown cold stare

I stood there

Looking pass the clouds and trees

Because in cosmic reality

I am a star seed,

LIFE

JANUARY 31, 2020

12:01 A.M.

Life is so extraordinary

Delightful and delicate

Heaven sent, as a resident,

It's evident that we seek thrills for the hell of it

Wild, crazy, dumb, or intelligent

Because in the back of everybody's mind

There a serial killer called Time

There is no running

He's already on your trail

And he is going to keep coming

This I promise

It is not a threat

Either live life to the fullest

Or die with regrets

SOUL

APRIL 1, 2020

6:41 P.M.

Soul, the immortal being

Inside the shell of flesh

The part of you that never dies

The only part that matters

The piece that is Godlike

Connected to your Master

The Most High

Some of them are honest

And others are demonic

Some of you don't have those

And some of you lost them

Some of you were cheap

And somebody bought them

The eyes are peepholes

Allowing you to see through people

Let them talk, and look directly in

Focus, don't blink

While they confess their sins

They sense something coming

And yes, they're afraid

Hell on Earth

Have you been living the right way?

Does your messy life need cleaning?

Or is it too late?

We are so deep in the matrix

Neo please awake

We are living in Revelation

Is there such a thing as satan

Excuse me

This topic had me thinking

My soul is precious

And everyone has a purpose

Can't keep curving it

Now is not the time to be nervous

TRUE COLORS

SEPTEMBER 10, 2022

3:10 P.M.

Some take longer than others

To see one's true colors

As long as you let them

They'll play you for a sucker

Pretending to be a friend, family, or brother

Your relationship can be an illusion

Based on the agenda of your significant other

For ten or fifteen minutes

Sit back and listen to them speak

They think they're running game

But they're exposing themselves

Can't manage their mouth

Won't stop flapping their cheeks

As for others, only time will tell

Pay attention to their detail

Could take weeks

But when that thread unravels

It's like a judge hitting the gavel

Guilty sentence

Looking silly

Can't believe you're finished

WITHDRAWALS

APRIL 4, 2022

11:00 P.M.

Most are only focused on their cause

When they need something is

The only time they call

Checking your account

Trying to make a withdrawal

Draining you of your motivation

And energy

But people never deposit

Back in to me

Low battery blinking red

In their mind, I am always positive

"He got plenty"

Negative! They don't know I'm overdrawn

About to shut down or how long I've been running on empty

I guess they figure I 'stay cooking'

So, I must have the recipe

Like a chef, can you assist

With the meal prep

Using and abusing me

For free therapy

SECRET FEELINGS

MARCH 28, 2022

9:39 P.M.

Vibes never lie

Secret feelings

Lead to public killings

Sometimes you can't see it coming

Because your coworker, family,

And friends be the villain

Plotting behind your back, wilding

You'll never know, because

They will be in your face, smiling

Pretending and practice grinning

The maestro orchestrating your ending

Hate you because they're not you

Mad stuck in the same place

They can't move

Be leery of those who offer you food

They might poison your plate

Now you're falling for their bait

Hook you like a fish and reel you in

To your death date

Some want you to expire

Others just want

To see you get fired

PERSONAL PROBLEMS

JULY 8, 2021

3:17 P.M.

If you have an issue with me

That I know nothing about

And you won't address it

But secretly, subliminally, silently

You're the one crying out

Sounds like a personal problem

Your wounds are self-inflicted

How do you expect to heal

When you won't treat it

Just keep picking it

Until it's bleeding

On everyone else

Even when I offer

You will not accept the help

Lost in your head emotional decisions

That's a single cell, a personal prison

In pieces pretending and grinning

Like rainbows, money, and unicorns

In the innermost center of your core

There's a storm

You can't seem to find shelter from

Hurt, hot, heated, angry, furious, fireball

Demonic demons slip in

You were vibrating low

Possessed off alcohol

Masking it with chronic but won't face it

Head-on reality is a bit much

Eating you up

Drink after drink, smoke after smoke

You chasing

Running, struggling, suffering, and aching

Frustrated trying to find your purpose and feeling basic

Until you get to the root of it

You will have a tree full of problems

That won't leave

NOTHING BUT THE BEST

APRIL 2, 2021

2:48 P.M.

I want to see you glow

So hard that it shines

Far beyond the globe

With a mindset of untold possibilities

Reaching every one of your goals

So, in your name, they dedicate facilities

Make movies in your honor

Sequels and trilogies

I wish you an abundance

Of positive energy

To be truthful

I just want to salute you

Good, great, joyful happiness

I want you to feel the opposite of numb

I want you to have the life you deserve

One you don't have to vacation from

KEEP AWAY

APRIL 15, 2023

1:08 PM

Just because your misery is lonely

And you're unhappy with yourself

You want the same fate for me

You want me to sip and die

As my dreams pass away

From drinking the same negative tea

The type of person who produces

Their own poison

Toxic flowing through their veins

It's sad, but your cells reject themselves

Maybe that's why

You can't comprehend or understand anything

Other than childish things

Off the Olympic diving board

You cannonball into a pool of liquor

Not quite as smart as Dr. Jekyll

Yet here comes Hyde

That was hiding in mister

Born with a virus

Emotional sickness

Throwing up how he really feel

Off the truth elixir

That's why I stay in my lane

Mind my business

And I don't fuck with ……

CLOWNZ

APRIL 3, 2021

5:21 P.M.

I know a clown

Who likes to parade around

In bright colors

I mean loud

Every day is a circus

Seeking attention from the crowd

Pure entertainment

Hopping out the car deep

Him and a group of dudes he hangs with

Wild in, but always smiling

Whatever, for some laughs

The more likes he gets

The better the clown feels

You do the math

Addition to all that subtracting

He can't figure out what he's lacking

He might have lost himself

Makeup plus mask times

How long he's been acting

Maybe the clown is starting to believe

I wonder if he knows they laugh at him

After he leaves

He's curious if they doubt him

He cares what they say about him

He's insecure about himself

Worrying over the thoughts

Of everyone else

An internal ocean waves of tears he cries

Coward scared to be his self

So every day he dies

RERUNS

MAY 14, 2022

9:31

In a *Full House*

I'm the *Fresh Prince*

Because I choose to think differently

I cut the wire and unplugged

From the program

Now *Boy Meets World*

Time for a *Home Improvement*

Society calls it *Criminal Mind*

I say, *I'm King Of The Hill*

They think they're *Saturday Night Live*

Doing the same thing over and over

Is annoying still

They love the *Matrix*, *Shameless*

I'm Neo and they are *Agents of S.H.I.E.L.D*

Animaniacs, *Rugrats*, and *Pretty Little Liars*

I'd rather be really *In Living Color*

Doing something that sets my soul on fire

At least give it a spark

They would rather stay in the dark

And figure out

How to Get Away with Murder

In *South Park*

It's a *Game Of Thrones* and

I have a story to tell

Saved By The Bell

When I checked out of

The *Bates Motel*

A MAN'S MENTAL HEALTH

SEPTEMBER 15, 2022

8:46 P.M.

You'll never know

What a man

Is going through

The infinite poker face

His hand

He'll never show you

I'M OKAY

DECEMBER 21, 2021

1:44 P.M.

When someone asks me

"Are you good?"

I can't complain

No one would listen

If I did anyway

Plus

It's not like I haven't been through this before

I keep my emotions bottled up

Trying not to pop my top

I'm a man, so I deal with

Can't confide or pour into anybody

They're messy, they spill quick

Kindly look you in your face

And see it as a weakness

Enthusiastic, ready to run

Their mouth like some sneakers

So I befriend the stress

And play with the pain

It won't last forever

It's just a little rain

EMOTIONAL SILENCE

MARCH 21, 2022

9:52 P.M.

I bottle up my emotions

Like I'm sailing out to sea

Throwing them deep in the

Ocean inside of me

Hidden stashed concealed

Hush hush

Die with my secrets

Because the living

You can not trust

It started when I was younger

When Pops ascended

I didn't know how to deal

With them

So I figured

I just kill them

Then it became a coping mechanism

Made life a lot easier

When your heart and feelings

Are locked in prison

Beware of those who swear

That with them, you can share

It's entrapment

Rubbing you on your back

While telling you it's ok

Then later on the phone

With their girlfriend laughing

So I carry the weight in silence

Everything except that

I am open-minded

DEPRESSION

(One of my first poems, but no date and time.)

Depression is silence

Isolation

Smiles and laughter

Just arrived

Yet when no one is looking

Leaves shortly after

Calls ignored—one-word text

Staying busy chasing checks

Seeking pleasure, avoiding pain

Covering wombs with drugs

And first-aid sex

You must heal and let it all out

But you're hiding and seeking

No one knows your whereabouts

Lying in the dark

Mentally ripping yourself apart

You stay together, so people can't tell

You're a man apart

Partial not whole

Stuck in a black hole

Exhausted, sick in the head, coughing

Tired

Just feel like taking a nap in a coffin

Out of my mind

Like the Headless Horseman, I lost it

War inside loaded with animosity and conflict

It's so easy to go back

To being a convict

True, if this mood were a color

It would be pale blue

With various shades of gray

Reminiscent of a dark, cloudy rainy day

SELF-DESTRUCT

JUNE 23, 2022

11:48 P.M.

It is so easy and simple to self-destruct

Just do nothing

float along the lazy river

Forfeiting is the same as giving up

No work or no participation

Is the same thing as not showing up

Loaded to the max

Stuck in

Refuse to move

Like the sick and shut-in

Taking up space

Wasting and rusting away

Your inner guide

Is mapping out directions everyday

But you ignore it

Like an annoyed mother

With a baby, who needs a break

Or a stepfather who is shady

Your inner child is crying

Because you're neglecting yourself

And not trying

SELF-BETRAYAL

APRIL 7, 2021

6:25 P.M.

Self-love's opponent is self-betrayal

Every time you *Judus* your inner *Jesus*

Your soul lives in hell

Anytime you forget your worth

Anytime you knowingly willingly

Let someone treat you like dirt

If your intuition, instinct, or gut

Says no, and you still do

Now you step into the shoes

Of Boo-Boo-the-Fool

Him I ain't

Putting myself second

On the back burner, I can't

ACCOUNTABILITY 2

MARCH 13, 2022

8:49 P.M.

At some point

You have to look in the mirror

Clean it, if it is foggy

To help you see clearer

Gaze deep into your eyes

And stare at yourself

Step back inhale

Take a deep breath

It took a deep dark tunnel

For me to see the light

My thinking was jacked up

I had to get my mind right

I felt so angry and so ashamed

When I realized every situation

Was my fault!

I was to blame

I had to stop trying

And start doing

Or

Other people's lives and mine

Would be ruined

Behind my bad habits

And toxic behavior

I had a choice to make

And I did

I became my own savior

L'S

MARCH 16, 2022

10:17 P.M.

Loser turned winner

Crawler to walker

Then a sprinter

No breakfast, no lunch

Just starving—then dinner

Loss after loss

L after L

Guess you can say

I was tripping because

It was fail after fail

When you lose *you*

Either you fold or give up

Or come back harder

You live, you learn

Hopefully, return smarter

Give it your all

Apply pressure

The only time it is truly over

Is when you are on a stretcher

Everyday above ground

Is a chance to get better

How bad do you want it?

Treat it like a vendetta

See a L is a blessing

Remove the B and ing

You are left with less

That in itself

Is a lesson

WAITING ON GOD

DECEMBER 5, 2022

5:32 P.M.

Waiting on God

I know a lot of people are

But what if he's waiting on you

What if she shows up

When you do?

Open up the heavens

And release the angels

As soon as you

Make the first move

Allah, universe, Jehovah, God favors risks

Whatever you call him

Whomever you pray to

When you're faced with a problem

God bless the child that

Can hold his own

Have faith even when alone

I take one step and she'll take ten

Outside, I was searching in the wrong place

Now I look within

Say grace ase'

I AM CAPABLE

JANUARY 10, 2023

11:46 P.M.

A warrior in a garden

No stainless

Calm and patient

Yet dangerous

Speechless

Not for a moment observing

Quiet by choice

Nor do I word search

I poetically word surf

More than a star

I AM made of them

I AM Mr. Universe

Every time I lost

A lesson was learned

Experience is effective

Useful, handy

Makes me qualified

To totally terminate

Any task I take on

Right, I remember

A rough life

Rich in knowledge

From early exposure

Maybe my memories

Made me

Proficient practice

From progressive participation

Prepares people or a person

To overcome any obstacle

Today's testimony will have you

Looking lucky later

Eager and enthusiastic

At every opportunity

All set regardless

No matter what I'm faced with

Whether it is classy or tasteless

At the top, breaking barriers

I've been in the basement

I can hear her calling

I am in love with destiny

Even as a child

She always got the best of me

I am one of the toughest

On the field

Where titans clash

Light work, no pressure

Just mental

There is nothing I can't handle

With a pen or a pencil

I AM the right utensil

HER LOVE STORY

MARCH 15, 2020

10:44 A.M.

When a little lady is born

They're taught to be Queens and Princesses

Wear dresses, cross legs take care of their body

Stay clean no messes

Spoiled by fathers

Watch out for wolves in sheep clothing

Cunning robbers who will rob her of her innocence

Trying to convince her, he is a charming prince

Blinded by the ignorance

That is bliss

Strapped with intelligence

She shot block

Controlling her biological clock

Dreams of story book weddings

Marrying a vet

Riding off into the sunset

Love at first site

Butterflies in the air

At the ball feeling like Cinderella tonight

Living Happily ever after, the perfect love

Any and all problems are solved

With a hug

But what if that's not real

No one is perfect

Programming filled with bullshit Injected

To your subconscious instilled

Reality is hard to swallow

Setup for failure a harsh pill

LADY IN DISGUISE

OCTOBER 8, 2022

11:56 P.M.

Her being screamed Goddess

Her beauty healed sore eyes

Her voice was soft

Seductive and sexy

Enough to make

A man's nature rise

She's a vibe that attracts

In the world not a care

What looked to be a

Pretty, peaceful world

Was a dungeon without pleasure

And the precious princess

Was a prisoner trapped there

Laughing and crying

At the same time

But the tears where invisible

Or maybe I was blind

She threw jokes

About a hell hole

Where she was forced to live

And on egg shells she tiptoe

Because one crack

Might disturb

The dangerous dragons nap

If he's not under the influence

It's useless, verbally abusive

The husband is going to snap

CONNECTION

FEBRUARY 4, 2024

11:15 A.M.

Soul connection

Passionate rhythm flexing

Inside a deep water well

Is where I dwell

Our souls unite

When our love fell

I never want to leave

Because here in this moment

We are free

ANIMATED

DECEMBER 18, 2019

11:05 P.M.

Walking through the forest like Hansel and Gretel

Knight in dull, damaged armor

You can hear my heavy metal

But beneath this exterior is a big bad wolf

Looking for Little Red Riding Hood

She doesn't have to be red

As long as she ride it good

Eat her into a coma

Look at her

My Sleeping Beauty is such a cutie

She yells when I Tinker her bell

That's how I know I hooked her captain

When Sheriff Woody is in the bedroom

It's time for some action

No toy story, I Buzz for a light year

She is my Cinderella and her

Prince Charming is right here

I'm gone off her Disney dizzy

Like Minnie slipped me a Mickey

Truthfully, we enjoy each other's company

Together we're goofy

Time stops when we enter Never Never Land

Where I butter and peter her pan

She had no panties on under that shirt

Window open it was Wendy

If I'm dreaming, don't pinch me

She lay back on the bed and told me Timon

Thought in my head, "Yeah it's on"

Pocahontas put my Symba on her Nala

This that ride off into the sunset

Not no forty dollar

Pouncing like Tigger

Pooh's honey went everywhere at the impact of climax

Her toes frozen, our souls glowing

No fairytale this was designed

By the divine we were chosen

COMMUNICATE DON'T CONVERSATE

NOVEMBER 11, 2022

9:46 A.M.

Everybody is conversating

But nobody is communicating

There is no exchange of information

They listen to the rebuttal

No one is receiving

Their plans, goals, and cause

Is the only things they believe in

I'm trying to plant a seed in your brain

But you're not conceiving

Why you can't hear me out

You only thinking about self

Is that your reason?

Each and every one is speaking

But we're not getting anywhere this evening

Argumentative, defensive, and deceiving

You are wasting my time

You might as well be thieving

Like a bad game of fetch

Because the message

You not retrieving

A CREATIVE FARMER

DECEMBER 20, 2022

1:06 A.M.

I remember a thought came to me

So I planted a seed

Over and over

Until it grew into a tree

See these branches

Didn't come from

The first seed

No instant gratification

No jack and the bean stalk

For me it took time

I didn't emerge from

The soil instantly

I had to nurture

Water and speak life into me

Open up the blinds

And let the sun shine in

You thought I was falling behind

But I was behind closed doors practicing

Perfecting a craft

That will eventually be

On autopilot doing math

No shade purposely

Money tree covers me

Intentionally

GIVING THANKS
NOVEMBER 24, 2022
11:12 A.M.

I'm blessed to be alive

I am thankful for family

But I can't let you forget

How this day came to be

Or for some, what it really means

Mid-evil suffering caused by Sergeant Slaughter

Toxic pain in the veins of indigenous people

Passed down trauma

Covered up your lies with fairytales

Hoping we forget the drama

Call it a holiday

YAY! Let us celebrate

Make them spend

On this holy day

Off the back end

We get paid

Let's also run sales

On Black Friday

Like we used to

In the slave trade

Yeah, you all are cold

Is it the people you killed

Or the land you stole?

What are you thankful for?

WHAT WOULD YOU DO

JANUARY 8, 2022

3:15 P.M.

If somebody chump you and your people

What would you do

Whether it was sneaking, backstabbing, or

In your face trucking like bump you

Mistreating handing out beatings

Being real unfair

Season after season

Playing like they care

But really misleading

You turn the other cheek

Wanting things to be cool

But the fire they keep feeding

Truckloads of gasoline

Playing you for a fool

Sticking you with no Vaseline

Mixing truth with lies

Selling wolf tickets and dreams

Setups and entrapments

Kidnapping and clapping

Hold the applause

I'm not laughing

You not tired of being a guinea pig

Getting slaughtered in the streets

Like a pig by a pig

Touch me it's going to be repercussions

Busting with no discussion

It's a time for everything

We talked and marched enough

Time to bring the pain

Take back what's ours

One unified gang

AMERIKKKA

AUGUST 15, 2023

11:40 A.M.

Every day I Geronimo"

Down a new rabbit hole

Sliding like hot butter

Right into the gutter

Coming the secret sewers

Full of lies and manure

Like a Ninja Turtle or Mario Bro

To uncover the truth

That lies beneath

The belly of the beast

On the surface

Picket fences make the estate

Look perfect

Nervous your alibi and get away

Are not so solid

Was it worth it

Crimes against the innocent

Kidnap torture

Rape and burn evidence

Kill and destroy your own people

Make right wrong and wrong legal

A superior Black Man was never meant

To be treated equal

A nigga for life is a

Nigga for lease

Never fails NFL

Or a Nigga in the streets

INJUSTICE

JUNE 27, 2020

5:08 P.M.

InjusticeThey are killing us!

Just cause

But the whole world

Is standing up

I am glad it's not just us

They been had their foot

On our necks

Videos show

They're not letting up

He smiled in the camera for ten minutes

While George Floyd couldn't breathe

"Don't shoot, hands up!"

Arms behind his back, handcuffed

The officer didn't aim and squeeze

He felt the need to use his knee

Killed this man in the street

For the whole world to see

Meanwhile, in Louisville, Kentucky

A set of different officers are using

Deadly force to the fullest degree

No knock warrant or warning

Just unload clips through the house

Once the gun smoke settled

Breonna Taylor was no longer

The LMPD had wrongfully took her out

"MEMORIAL DAY"

MAY 30, 2021

11:41 A.M.

See one fights battles everyday

That's why before you go to sleep

And if the most high allows you to awake

You should pray

That you're covered and smothered

In the all knowing protection and glory

Because in a lifetime there are many wars

In her or his story

You can't win them all

But you must learn from each

To prepare for the next brawl

In your mind they're a friend of me

Awareness is key

It is essential to know thy enemy

To risky to be lead by the blind

Or following behind blindly

And you most definitely

Cannot fight ferocious kindly

See to me a soldier has no limits

Relaxed and calm never timid

Courageous cut from God's cloth

No gimmicks soul different

Warrior spirit

Previous past warfare made him smarter

Now he adapt and slide like water

No matter what he facing

He must make modifications

For any occasion

Do what needs to be done

Whether its kill or spare one

Weed out the spies

Watch for the double cross

And listen for the lies

Don't get lost

At no time not ever roll over

This is my tribute and salute

To the fallen soldier

LABOR DAY

SEPTEMBER 5, 2022

4:51 P.M.

Ha labor day

These folks who pay

For labor play

Play petty

Play with your check

Can't understand why

You are getting upset

By the way

Could you stay over

And do another set

Working for paper

That comes from the trees

It all comes from nature

Everything is free

As far as the

Eye can see

Got us running a rat's race

Chasing cheese

For basic needs

It's not a secret

That's not the way

It's supposed to be

I feel like it's a toxic relationship

And you're controlling me

"BLACK HISTORY"

FEBRUARY 25, 2021

7:43 P.M.

Melanin is found

All throughout the universe

Woven all in between the weave

Of Mother Earth

It's not a mystery

We are world history

Picked apart by vultures

Look beneath the surface

We are hidden in every culture

Shaping the globe

Like a sculpture

On every street

Mud or concrete

On every corner

Every crack

Big brands primetime

Commercial marketing

All you see is Black Royalty

Used to make revenue

Liquor and raw recipes

Opposite day rescued

From colored women and dudes

Who once used to rule

Yet now gunned down

And treated like mules

Until worthless

And out of fuel

Get up again and again

Take it on the chin

Let it roll off your back

No matter how cruel

Still, we smile

The days we brighten

Inspire and enlighten

For this reason, we walk

Through the valley of death

Even if we're frightened

Building with purpose

This is God writing

www.ingramcontent.com/pod-product-compliance
Lightning Source LLC
Chambersburg PA
CBHW051659090426
42736CB00013B/2455